To the

third and fourth

Generation!

i

Also by Dr. Gwynn

Easter-Not What You Think

Chrislam – What Communion Hath Light With Darkness?

Conflict – Christianity's Love vs. Islam's Submission

The President Was a Good Man

Anything for Acceptance

Healing – The Children's Bread

Created to Live!

The gods Among Us

Bless and Curse Not!

To the

third and fourth

Generation!

Dr. Murl Edward Gwynn

Published by MEG Enterprises Publications
PO Box 2165
Reidsville, GA 30453
(912) 557-6507
meg@kencable.net
www.murlgwynn.com

Unless otherwise identified, Scripture quotations are from
the Holy Bible New International Version, copyright ©
1973, 1978, 1984 by International Bible Society.
Zondervan Publishing House. Used by permission.

Scripture quotations marked KJV are from the King James
Version of the Bible.

Printed in the U.S.A by

International Standard Book Number: 978-0-9862596-0-9

TABLE OF CONTENTS

ACKNOWLEDGMENTS

Ruth, my best friend and only wife!

PREFACE

In my ministry for the past thirty six years I have taught and heard many Christians speak of ancestral curses.

Those curses were supposedly passed down from our ancestors who did not follow God and rebelled against the things and ways of God.

The results of those curses came to be the dark and deciding factor in many of our sickness, problems, and negative lifestyles; or so we thought! In these later years I have come to realize my ignorance in the belief of ancestral cursings.

What we have come to accept as ancestral cursing's is no more than lifestyles that either refuse to accept responsibility or try to blame others for our sin or shortcomings.

By no means am I suggesting that people who are honestly seeking relief or rest from nagging problems won't accept responsibility, although many don't. I am suggesting that we have taught and believed something that is just not taught in scripture.

I am guilty of teaching a falsehood, not as a charlatan, by in ignorance. I wanted to help, but I'm afraid I missed the mark!

Be that as it may, it is time we look honestly at the subject of sin/sins being passed down to the third and fourth generations.

1 - Why

Many people do not realize that they are beneficiaries of blessing or curse. Whether we receive blessing or curse can depend on how we live our lives and, also, what we learned from our fathers and mothers. Sadly, many people walk in curses when they could walk in blessings.

God warns mankind to be circumspect[1] as to how we live our lives. If we walk in obedience to God's commands and set standards we will

---

[1] Circumspect: careful to consider all circumstances and consequences, PRUDENT

realize growth, prosperity, and health. If we walk contrary to the natural and spiritual laws of God we will reap discord in all forms.

It must be understood that God's creation, whether in the physical or spiritual realm, is made to function according to laws that govern its growth and wellbeing. If those laws are broken there is sickness, failure, or discord. If those laws are followed there is health, success, and order. The choice is mans!

Sins follow

God tells us in scripture that sins follow a people even down through the generations.

You shall not bow down to them or worship them; for I, the Lord your God, am a jealous God, punishing the children for the sin of the fathers to the third and fourth generation of those who hate me, but showing love to a thousand [generations] of those who love me and keep my commandments. "You shall not misuse the name of the Lord your God, for the Lord will not hold anyone guiltless who misuses his name Exodus 20:5-7

Why would God punish the sins of the fathers on the children? The answer to that question isn't as tricky as one would imagine.

First we must understand some principles of God and spiritual flow.

NOTE ONE:

It must be kept in mind that the verses in Exodus 20: 5-7 are speaking of one specific people, the Hebrews that worship idols and hate God. It is to them God is speaking and warning of visiting the sins of the fathers down to the third and fourth generations.

NOTE TWO:

God gives us specific information about the sins of the father and their children. In Ezekiel 18:19-20 it states *"Yet you say, 'Why should the son not bear the guilt of the father?' Because the son has done what is lawful and right, and has kept all My statutes and observed them, he shall surely live. The soul who sins shall die. The son shall not bear the guilt of the father, nor the father bear the guilt of the son. The righteousness of the righteous shall be upon himself, and the wickedness of the wicked shall be upon himself.* Therefore, we must always remember that God does not visit the sins of the father down to the third and fourth generation unless those generations are idol worshippers and haters of God as stated in

3

Exodus 20:5-7 which makes sense since it is their own sins which are being visited upon them and they would be under the curse.

MAN THE LAW-BREAKER

Man is the great law-breaker, and he must reap what he sows. Man is responsible in the first place for yielding to sin and Satan and submitting to demon powers that take advantage of his sinful state and cause all kinds of failures and sufferings in his life. He is responsible for breaking God's laws; for living in lusts and uncleanness, which breeds sickness and disease; for accidents due to careless living; for lack of power from God to defeat Satan; for lack of proper exercise; for failure to keep the body in a clean, healthy state; for overwork and intemperance in eating, in drinking, and in proper care of the body; for the wrong use of his faculties, which cause worry and fear that tear down natural and spiritual resistance to sickness; for certain conditions that pass on from one generation to another; and for failure to appropriate the benefits for which Jesus died so that he can be healed and delivered from satanic powers. Sins of all kinds, rebellion, and misuse of the tongue, hardness of heart, fleshly lusts, pride, unbelief, and many other personal acts on the part of men have caused them to break the laws of God and give the agents of sin, sickness, and death the opportunity to bring about sickness in their lives. This vulnerability does not mean that demons always take advantage at once, for sometimes it is to their advantage not to use their powers to bring sickness upon the law-breakers. But eventually those who sow will have to reap.

When the Bible says that God puts physical sickness and disease upon men, as in the following Scriptures, it simply means that His law of sowing and reaping is being executed by the proper agencies to enforce this law (Exod. 15:26; Deut. 7:15; 28:1-68). In these passages it is stated that sickness is the result of sowing sin. If there had been no sin there would have been no disease. In many places where it speaks of God taking a certain action, in reality He used proper agents actually to bring it to pass. It is said that God sent Joseph into Egypt, but in reality his brethren were the ones who sold him to the Ishmaelites (Gen. 45:4-8). It is said that God would visit Israel and lead them out of Egypt, but in reality God used Moses and Aaron as his agents to do this (Gen. 50:24; Ps. 77:20). It is said on numerous occasions that God subdued Israel's enemies, but in reality He used human agency to do it (Judg. 4:14-23). The same is true of the law of sickness and disease. He has given the actual power of this law into the hands of demon powers.

Sins of repetition

We often hear someone who is going through a family repeated cycle of familiar negatives mention that they believe they are under the curse that was passed down from their ancestors. As we have seen about the sins of the fathers to the children this is obviously not true; it most likely is a lifestyle that has been learned from generation to generation.

Yes, there are physical sickness and emotional problems that come from our ancestors, but this is not the passing down of sins, it is most likely the general original sin of

6

Adam and the fall of mankind in the Garden of Eden. When Adam sinned all of the genetic properties of mankind in Adam came to all humankind and for that reason our bodies, emotions, and genetic makeup are perceptible to sicknesses of all kinds. Some family's physical makeup is more perceptible to certain stimuli than others.

However, these so called 'sins of repetition' seem to hang on in many families for generations and become a sad, but, normative way of life and a constant source of discouragement and pain until they are broken by someone in the family who turns to the Lord. Often these families see these problems as a curse mentioned in Exodus 20:5-7, but in all reality they are not. In the next chapter we will discuss the breaking of curses.

2 - Breaking of curse

The topic of 'breaking of curses' is a touchy subject in many circles in Christianity. There are many well-known ministers who teach that the church should always break ancestor curses when dealing with someone who goes through family and individual problems. These ministers, I believe, are well meaning and want the best for those they are ministering to, but I believe we must be careful to always teach and minister according to scripture and the example of Jesus and the early church disciples.

I find no place in the New Testament that either Jesus or His disciples broke curse over anyone they were ministering to. From sickness or demon possession neither our Lord nor an Apostle saw fit to break an ancestor curse over anyone. They either spoke healing or demanded demons to leave with nothing more than the authority given to them and faith; in Jesus' case, authority from the Father, and in the disciple's case, the authority given by Jesus.

Free from the curse

Every person who turns to the Lord repents of their sins, and follows Jesus is free from any curse. They are removed from the curse of the law, the general curse of the original sin, and any curse that the enemy tries to bring.

God makes it very clear that anyone who is in Christ Jesus is not under any type of curse. *Gal 3:13-14 Christ has redeemed us from the curse of the law, having become a curse for us (for it is written, "Cursed is everyone who hangs on a tree"), that the blessing of Abraham might come upon the Gentiles in Christ Jesus, that we might receive the promise of the Spirit through faith.* Therefore, anyone who is in Christ Jesus does not have to be concerned about any curse.

When Adam and Eve sinned in the Garden of Eden they turned the rule-ship and subduing of the earth they received from God to Satan. Before the sin everything was good and blessed. After the sin everything, under the new rule-ship of Satan, brought curse upon the earth. It must be understood that it was not God who cursed the earth, it was Adam. God does not bless anything of rebellion, and what He doesn't bless falls under the curse of Adam and Satan's corruption.

For the Christian there would be no cause for a curse to come upon them or have any power to affect them. The curse of the law, the curse of sin, and the curse of corruption has been broken by what Jesus did on the cross. There would be no cause for a curse to affect the Saints of God. *Like a flitting sparrow, like a flying swallow, so a curse without cause shall not alight. Prov 26:2*

For someone to claim that they are struggling with an ancestral curse would be doubting what Jesus did for them on the cross. What Jesus did on the cross set all of mankind

free from the effect of sin's power! Through the
first Adam sin entered all of creation, bringing
death, destruction, and fear. The curse of
corruption came upon everything. But, Jesus'
sacrifice, as the final representative of mankind,
broke the curse in all forms and made those who
accept that fact free from them. There would be
no cause for any curse to affect the saint.

Free from condemnation

*There is therefore now no condemnation to those
who are in Christ Jesus, who do not walk according to the
flesh, but according to the Spirit. For the law of the Spirit
of life in Christ Jesus has made me free from the law of sin
and death. For what the law could not do in that it was
weak through the flesh, God did by sending His own Son in
the likeness of sinful flesh, on account of sin: He
condemned sin in the flesh, that the righteous requirement
of the law might be fulfilled in us who do not walk
according to the flesh but according to the Spirit. Rom 8:1-
4*

We must never forget that there is nothing
to condemn the saint for. When Jesus went to
the cross, paid the penalty for sins rebellion, and
was cursed on our behalf, no curse can affect us
in any form or realm.

Condemnation can only come to those
who are guilty of a crime or fault. Since the saint

is the recipient of Jesus' righteous act of sacrifice, we stand as if we are justified and free from sins punishment.

The Christian is now a recipient of the righteous requirement of the law that demands that those who are righteous must receive righteous rewards. Those rewards are blessing and not curse. Just as it was intended before the sin of Adam in the Garden of Eden!

The true breaking of curse lies with Jesus, the one and only curse breaker. Every curse, every sin, and every anti-God rebellion was put upon our savior who made us free from the curse and has made us sons/daughters of blessing.

3 - Justified

Behold what manner of love the Father has bestowed on us, that we should be called children of God! Therefore the world does not know us, because it did not know Him. 2 Beloved, now we are children of God; and it has not yet been revealed what we shall be, but we know that when He is revealed, we shall be like Him, for we shall see Him as He is. 3 And everyone who has this hope in Him purifies himself, just as He is pure. 1 John 3:1-3

Justification is the **work of God where** the righteousness of Jesus is reckoned to the sinner, so the sinner is declared by God as being righteous under the Law (Rom. 4:3; 5:1,9; Gal. 2:16; 3:11). **This righteousness is** not earned or retained by any effort of the saved. Justification is an instantaneous occurrence with the result being eternal life. It is based completely and solely upon Jesus' sacrifice on the cross (1 Pet. 2:24) and is received by faith alone (Eph. 2:8-9). No works are necessary whatsoever to obtain justification. Otherwise, it is not a gift (Rom. 6:23). Therefore, we are **justified by faith (Romans 5:1)**.

As shared in the last chapter, the Christian is not under any condemnation or considered guilty of sin anymore because of what Jesus did on the cross. Jesus took our sins, made us son/daughters of God, and made it possible for the promises made to Abraham, and then to Jesus to come to us. We, through faith in what Jesus did, are recipients of the promises.

The Christian, as a child of God is put into the position of honor, respect, authority, and separation.

In respect to honor; each person who repents of sins, accepts the sacrifice of Jesus, and believes that God sent His Son is now *honored* to be a citizen of heaven and the kingdom of God. He/she is made just-as-if they were always in that honored position.

With this honor one now can walk in the reality of Jesus' prayer mentioned in Matthew 6:9-13[2]. Since it is God's will for that which is in

---

[2]Matt 6:9-13 - In this manner, therefore, pray: Our Father in heaven, Hallowed be Your name. 10 Your kingdom come. Your will be done on earth as it is in heaven. 11 Give us this day our daily bread. 12 And forgive us our debts, as we forgive our debtors. 13 And do not lead us

heaven to be flowing in the earth, it is through His children that those realities manifest. His will is accomplished through His children! His children are those who have been justified through Jesus!

In respect to *respect*; each child of God who walks in the understanding of the sacrifice of Jesus and knows through faith the power in that name must be respected by powers and principalities.

In respect to authority; Jesus gave God's children the authority to speak on His behalf, cast out demons, heal the sick, and preform those things Jesus did. This authority proves God's love, mercy, and forgiveness towards mankind through the Son.[3]

---

into temptation, But deliver us from the evil one. For Yours is the kingdom and the power and the glory forever. Amen. NKJV

[3] Mark 16:15-18 And He said to them, "Go into all the world and preach the gospel to every creature. 16 He who believes and is baptized will be saved; but he who does not believe will be condemned. 17 And these signs will follow those who believe: In My name they will cast out demons; they will speak with new tongues; 18 they will take up serpents; and if they drink anything deadly, it will by no means hurt them; they will lay hands on the sick, and they will recover." NKJV

In respect to separation; each child of God has been made separate from the world. They can function in both the world and heavenly realms, but they, through faith, are made separate onto God for good works.[4]

We can see then, because we are justified by God through Jesus we are not under any kind of curse, bondage, or ancestral baggage. We have been justified and freed from those things our ancestors may have been rebellious too.

Abraham's blessing given to Jesus and then us!

As stated earlier, the child of God has been justified through Jesus' sacrifice. The Christian is not under any kind of curse and is free to live according to God's pleasure, power, and direction. What God intended for mankind in the Garden of Eden has been fulfilled in Jesus!

When God found a man, Abraham, he found a man who would walk in faith. God made promises to Abraham because He wanted to

---

[4] Eph 2:10 For we are His workmanship, created in Christ Jesus for good works, which God prepared beforehand that we should walk in them. NKJV

bless all of mankind through the power of faith which Abraham was an example of.

Abraham's blessing entailed a three part blessing; personal, national, and global.

Gal 3:14 that the blessing of Abraham might come upon the Gentiles in Christ Jesus, that we might receive the promise of the Spirit through faith.

Personal blessing:

Abraham's personal blessing from God touched Abraham's wealth, his offspring, and his intimate relationship with God Himself.

Jesus fulfilled everything that God promised Abraham, thereby receiving the ancient blessing and making it possible for all those who would walk in faith to receive them as well.

National blessing:

Abraham's national blessing from God would touch the nations which would flow from Abraham. His offspring would realize prosperity and peace if they walked in the same faith of Abraham.

This national blessing touched the Jews, the offspring of Abraham, and through them the word of God would come, the reality of God's presence in the earth, and the child from who all blessings would flow; Jesus.

Global blessing:

Before Jesus came to be the perfect sacrifice for sin only the Jews were considered recipients of God's promises, but because of Jesus those promises are now available to every human; the gentiles.

The promise is fully realized by the Holy Spirit given to those who would respond to the gift of salvation made possible by Jesus.

Every person, in any part of the world is called to be a recipient of the promised Holy Spirit and the fulfillment of the blessing of Abraham through Christ Jesus.

Therefore there is no curse, no condemnation to them who are in Christ Jesus. There is no ancestral curse over any person who turns to the Lord and walks in the blessings of Christ!

PERIOD!

www.ingramcontent.com/pod-product-compliance
Lightning Source LLC
Chambersburg PA
CBHW060706280326
41933CB00012B/2329